Postkarten

VUES D'EN HAUT
30 cartes postales
uniques

© 2000 Copyright for this postcard book:
New Internationalist Publications Ltd, Oxford, www.newint.org

Design by Barbara Willi, Zurich, Switzerland.
British Library Cataloguing-in-Publication Data.
A catalogue record for this book is available from the British Library.

ISBN 1 869847 93 8

Printed by C&C Offset Printing Co. Ltd., Hong Kong

From the book
"The Earth from the Air"
Thames & Hudson, London,
1999
© for photographs rests with
Yann Arthus-Bertrand,
Impact Pictures.
All rights reserved.

Aus dem Buch
«Die Erde von oben»
GEO im Verlag Gruner+Jahr
AG & Co., Hamburg, 1999
© Fotografie:
Yann Arthus-Bertrand,
Impact Pictures.
Alle Rechte vorbehalten.

De l'ouvrage
«La Terre vue du ciel»
paru aux Editions de
La Martinière, Paris, 1999
© Photographie:
Yann Arthus-Bertrand,
agence Altitude.
Tous droits réservés.

VIEWS FROM ABOVE

These extraordinary postcards have been specially selected from the book "The Earth from the Air" – itself an extraordinary visual record of the state of the world's environment. Internationally-acclaimed French photographer Yann Arthus-Bertrand flew over 60 countries to capture landscapes, dwellings, coasts, forests and animals, providing a unique showcase of the Earth. Many images reveal the imprint of human civilisation on the face of the globe, and so they also record the impact of population and the world industrial economy.

Arthus-Bertrand's lens finds human settlements, forests, islands, rivers and deserts in extraordinary compositions of light and form. Often taken from low altitude the images reveal people, animals and many other details, making a scene come alive. In these panoramas of wide vistas and intimate glimpses of tiny features, Arthus-Bertrand's photos have opened a remarkable window on the Earth.

BILDER AUS DER LUFT

30 ausgewählte Sujets aus dem Buch «Die Erde von oben» als Postkarten. Der renommierte Fotograf Yann Arthus-Bertrand überflog mehr als 60 Länder, um Landschaften, Küsten, Behausungen, Wälder und Tiere aus ungewohnter Perspektive festzuhalten. Im fesselnden Spiel mit Licht und Formen und aus geringer Höhe fotografiert, erwachen überraschende Details zum Leben und vermitteln neuartige Einblicke in die Kultur und das Leben der Menschen. Arthus-Bertrands Aufnahmen aus der Luft zeugen aber auch von den negativen Auswirkungen der von Industrialisierung und Modernisierung geprägten Gesellschaft. Entstanden ist ein einzigartiges visuelles Porträt unseres Planeten.

VUES D'EN HAUT

30 sujets extraits de l'ouvrage «La Terre vue du ciel», en cartes postales. Le photographe renommé Yann Arthus-Bertrand a survolé plus de soixante pays pour fixer, depuis une perspective inhabituelle, les campagnes, les côtes, l'habitat, les forêts et les animaux. Dans le jeu fascinant des lumières et des formes, photographiées à faible hauteur, des détails surprenants s'éveillent à la vie et éclairent d'un jour nouveau la vie des hommes et leurs cultures. Les vues aériennes d'Arthus-Bertrand mettent aussi en évidence les blessures infligées par l'industrialisation et la modernisation. Un portrait visuel unique en son genre de notre planète.

▶ NEW INTERNATIONALIST ▶ WWW.NEWINT.ORG ▶ HELVETAS ▶ WWW.HELVETAS.CH
▶ WHITE HAVEN'S BEACH ▶ QUEENSLAND ▶ AUSTRALIA
▶ WHITE HAVEN'S BEACH ▶ QUEENSLAND ▶ AUSTRALIEN
▶ WHITE HAVEN'S BEACH ▶ QUEENSLAND ▶ AUSTRALIE ▶ PHOTO: YANN ARTHUS-BERTRAND

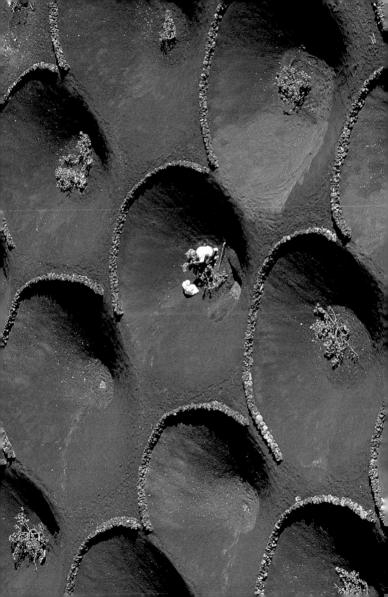

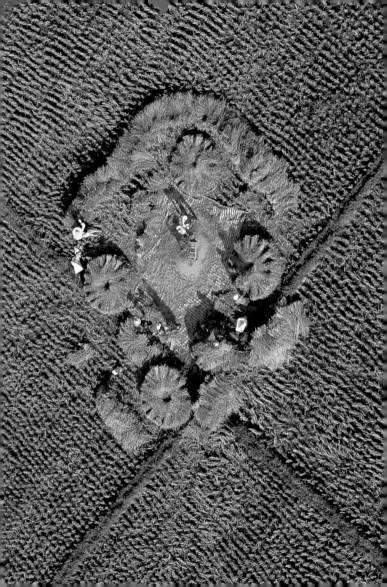

▶ NEW INTERNATIONALIST ▶ WWW.NEWINT.ORG ▶ HELVETAS ▶ WWW.HELVETAS.CH
▶ RICE HARVESTING ▶ CHIANG MAI ▶ THAILAND
▶ REISERNTE ▶ CHIANG MAI ▶ THAILAND
▶ TRAVAUX DES CHAMPS ▶ CHIANG MAI ▶ THAILANDE ▶ PHOTO: YANN ARTHUS-BERTRAND

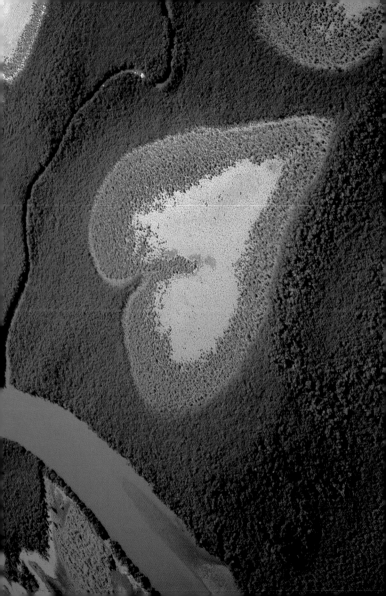

▶ NEW INTERNATIONALIST ▶ WWW.NEWINT.ORG ▶ HELVETAS ▶ WWW.HELVETAS.CH
▶ MANGROVE SWAMP ISLET ▶ VOH ▶ NEW CALEDONIA
▶ MANGROVEN-HERZ ▶ VOH ▶ NEUKALEDONIEN
▶ LE CŒUR DE VOH ▶ NOUVELLE-CALÉDONIE ▶ PHOTO: YANN ARTHUS-BERTRAND

▶ NEW INTERNATIONALIST ▶ WWW.NEWINT.ORG ▶ HELVETAS ▶ WWW.HELVETAS.CH
▶ BODNATH BUDDHIST TEMPLE ▶ KATMANDU ▶ NEPAL
▶ DER STUPA VON BODNATH ▶ TAL VON KATMANDU ▶ NEPAL
▶ LE STÛPA DE BODNATH ▶ KATMANDOU ▶ NÉPAL ▶ PHOTO: YANN ARTHUS-BERTRAND

▶ NEW INTERNATIONALIST ▶ WWW.NEWINT.ORG ▶ HELVETAS ▶ WWW.HELVETAS.CH
▶ ISLET ▶ SULU ARCHIPELAGO ▶ PHILIPPINES
▶ INSEL ▶ SULU-ARCHIPEL ▶ PHILIPPINEN
▶ ILOT ▶ ARCHIPEL DE SULU ▶ PHILIPPINES ▶ PHOTO: YANN ARTHUS-BERTRAND

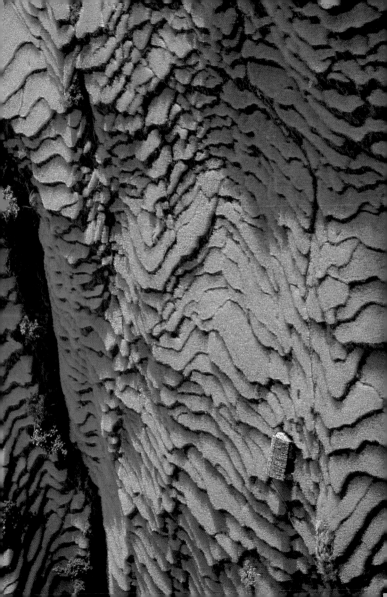

▶ NEW INTERNATIONALIST ▶ WWW.NEWINT.ORG ▶ HELVETAS ▶ WWW.HELVETAS.CH
▶ RICE PADDIES ▶ GANDAK ▶ NEPAL
▶ REISFELDER ▶ GANDAK ▶ NEPAL
▶ RIZIÈRES ▶ GANDAK ▶ NÉPAL ▶ PHOTO: YANN ARTHUS-BERTRAND

▶ NEW INTERNATIONALIST ▶ WWW.NEWINT.ORG ▶ HELVETAS ▶ WWW.HELVETAS.CH
▶ GUGGENHEIM MUSEUM ▶ BILBAO ▶ SPAIN
▶ GUGGENHEIM-MUSEUM ▶ BILBAO ▶ SPANIEN
▶ MUSÉE GUGGENHEIM ▶ BILBAO ▶ ESPAGNE ▶ PHOTO: YANN ARTHUS-BERTRAND

► NEW INTERNATIONALIST ► WWW.NEWINT.ORG ► HELVETAS ► WWW.HELVETAS.CH
► ST SOPHIA MOSQUE ► ISTANBUL ► TURKEY
► HAGIA SOPHIA ► ISTANBUL ► TÜRKEI
► BASILIQUE SAINTE-SOPHIE ► ISTANBUL ► TURQUIE ► PHOTO: YANN ARTHUS-BERTRAND

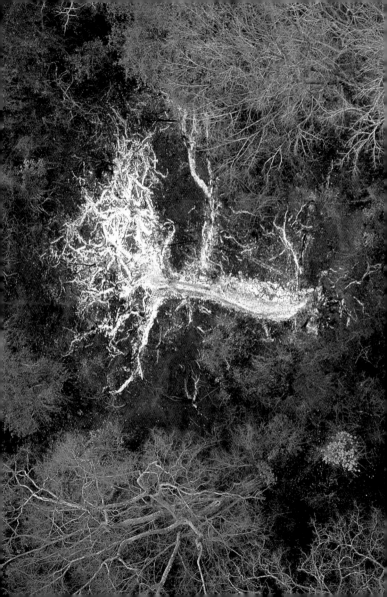

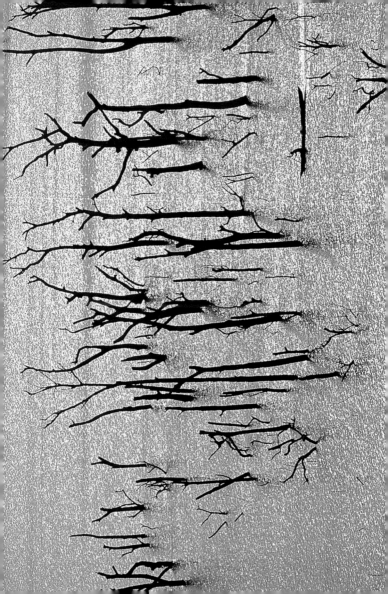

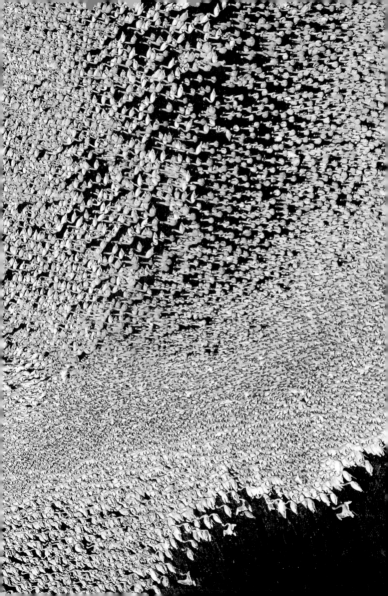

▶ NEW INTERNATIONALIST ▶ WWW.NEWINT.ORG ▶ HELVETAS ▶ WWW.HELVETAS.CH
▶ PINK FLAMINGOS ▶ LAKE NAKURU ▶ KENYA
▶ FLAMINGOS ▶ NAKURUSEE ▶ KENIA
▶ FLAMANTS ROSES ▶ LAC NAKURU ▶ KENYA ▶ PHOTO: YANN ARTHUS-BERTRAND

▶ NEW INTERNATIONALIST ▶ WWW.NEWINT.ORG ▶ HELVETAS ▶ WWW.HELVETAS.CH
▶ SUNSET OVER MANHATTAN ▶ NEW YORK ▶ UNITED STATES
▶ SONNENUNTERGANG ÜBER MANHATTAN ▶ NEW YORK ▶ USA
▶ COUCHER DE SOLEIL SUR MANHATTAN ▶ NEW YORK ▶ USA ▶ PHOTO: YANN ARTHUS-BERTRAND

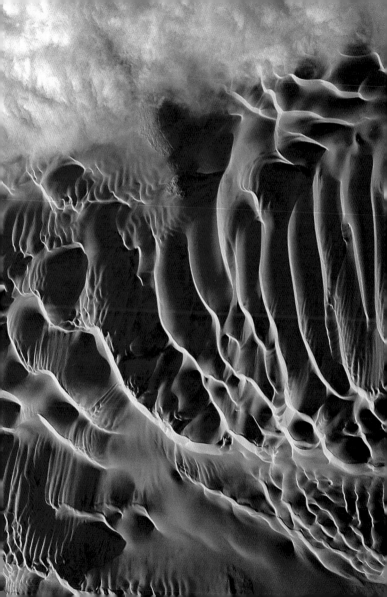

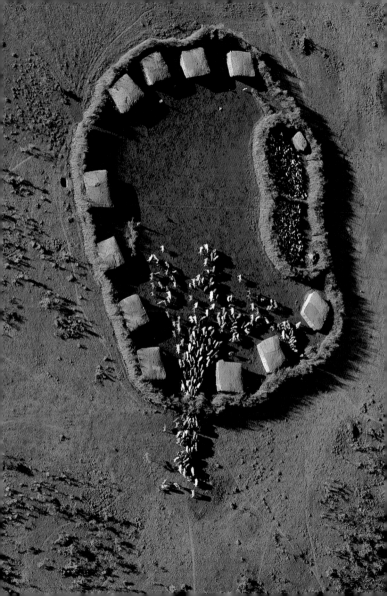

▶ NEW INTERNATIONALIST ▶ WWW.NEWINT.ORG ▶ HELVETAS ▶ WWW.HELVETAS.CH
▶ ROWING BOATS ▶ LIMA ▶ PERU
▶ RUDERBOOTE ▶ LIMA ▶ PERU
▶ BARQUES ▶ LIMA ▶ PÉROU ▶ PHOTO: YANN ARTHUS-BERTRAND

▶ NEW INTERNATIONALIST ▶ WWW.NEWINT.ORG ▶ HELVETAS ▶ WWW.HELVETAS.CH
▶ LANDSCAPE OF ICE ▶ NUNAVUT TERRITORY ▶ CANADA
▶ EISFELDER ▶ NUNAVUT-GEBIET ▶ KANADA
▶ PAYSAGE DE GLACE ▶ TERRITOIRE NUNAVUT ▶ CANADA ▶ PHOTO: YANN ARTHUS-BERTRAND

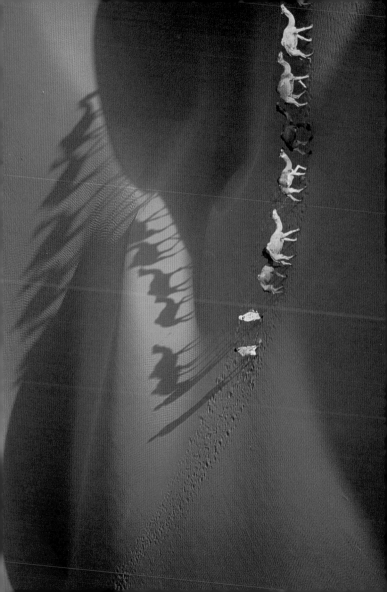

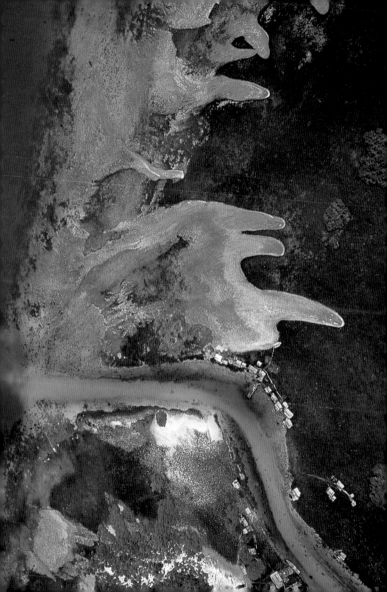

► NEW INTERNATIONALIST ► WWW.NEWINT.ORG ► HELVETAS ► WWW.HELVETAS.CH
► HOUSE AMID RICE TERRACES ► BALI ► INDONESIA
► VON REISTERRASSEN UMGEBENES HAUS ► BALI ► INDONESIEN
► ILOT DANS LES RIZIÉRES EN TERRASSES ► BALI ► INDONÉSIE ► PHOTO: YANN ARTHUS-BERTRAND

For further details on New Internationalist magazine, publications and products please contact:

▶ **UNITED KINGDOM AND EUROPE**
New Internationalist
55 Rectory Road
Oxford OX4 1BW
United Kingdom
Tel: 01865 728181

▶ **UNITED STATES**
New Internationalist
P O Box 1143
Lewiston
NY 14092
USA
Tel: (800) 661 8700

▶ **CANADA**
New Internationalist
P O Box 706
Markham
Ontario
L6B 1A7
Canada
Tel: (905) 946 0407

▶ **AUSTRALIA AND PNG**
New Internationalist
28 Austin Street
Adelaide
S.A. 5000
Australia
Tel: (08) 8232 1563

▶ **AOTEAROA/NEW ZEALAND**
New Internationalist
P O Box 4499
Christchurch
Aotearoa/New Zealand
Tel: +(03) 3656 153

YANN ARTHUS-BERTRAND, the world-famous French photographer, began his career in conservation. While living in Africa he took many pictures of lions in Kenya's Masai-Mara nature reserve, resulting in his first photographic book, "Lions" (1983). It was in Africa too that he started what has become his speciality – aerial photography. Floating above the landscape in a hot-air balloon, he discovered a different beauty in the world.

On returning to France Arthus-Bertrand became a professional photographer, following the Paris-Dakar races and continuing his wildlife interests. In 1991 he founded the Altitude agency in Paris, where he lives. His books include "Greece from the Air" (1998), "New York from the air" (1997) and "Good Breeding" (1999). Arthus-Bertrand's photos appear in magazines such as *National Geographic*, *Life*, *Geo* and *Paris Match*.

YANN ARTHUS-BERTRAND, 1946 in Frankreich geboren, gilt als einer der besten Luftbildfotografen der Welt. Entdeckt hat er diese Leidenschaft während einer Ballonfahrt über die Savanne Kenias, als er beauftragt war, die Löwen des Masai-Mara-Naturreservats zu fotografieren. Die Aufnahmen wurden 1983 in seinem ersten Fotoband «Lions» veröffentlicht. Mehr als die Löwen faszinierte ihn allerdings die neue Perspektive auf eine Landschaft, die sich ihm erst von oben betrachtet in ihrer ganzen Schönheit offenbarte. 1991 gründete er in Paris die Agentur Altitude. Als einzige der Welt hat sie sich ausschliesslich auf Luftbildaufnahmen von Ländern, Landschaften und Kulturen spezialisiert. Arthus-Bertrands Bilder sind in zahlreichen Zeitschriften wie *National Geographic*, *Life*, *Geo* und *Paris Match* erschienen. Der Fotograf lebt in Paris.

YANN ARTHUS-BERTRAND, né en France en 1946, découvre sa passion pour la photographie aérienne lors d'un vol en ballon à l'occasion d'un reportage sur les lions de la réserve naturelle de Masai-Mara au Kenya. Ses photos ont paru en 1983 dans «Lions», son premier album. Plus que les lions, cependant, ce sont les perspectives nouvelles, offertes par la beauté des paysages vus du ciel qui le fascinèrent. En 1991, il crée à Paris l'agence Altitude, première agence au monde spécialisée dans la photographie aérienne des paysages et des cultures. Les photographies de Yann Arthus-Bertrand ont été publiées dans de nombreux magazines, tels que *National Geographic*, *Life*, *Geo* et *Paris Match*. Le photographe vit à Paris.